Russell Stannard

The Lab Cats On the Move

A look at what makes things move

Illustrated by
Bill Ledger

MARSHALL PUBLISHING · LONDON

Note to Parents

This **Lab Cats** book introduces the idea of what makes things move. Children come to understand the concept through the adventures of a gang of cats. The book can be read aloud while a younger child follows the words and pictures, or an older child can read it alone. Each experiment that the cats do is followed by the correct answers. Ask your child to give the answer before turning the page to see what the Lab Cats did. Any new or difficult scientific words are explained in "What the Words Mean" on page 36. Happy reading!

A Marshall Edition
Conceived, edited and designed by
Marshall Editions Ltd
The Orangery
161 New Bond Street
London W1S 2UF
www.marshallpublishing.com

First published in the UK in 2001 by
Marshall Publishing Ltd

10 9 8 7 6 5 4 3 2 1

ISBN 1 84028 546 X

Originated in the UK by Hilo
Printed in Portugal by Printer Portuguesa

Editor: Rosalind Beckman
Managing Designer: Caroline Sangster
Art Director: Simon Webb
Editorial Manager: Janet Sacks
US Consultant: Dr Roberta Butler
Production: Christina Schuster

During the day, the school cat roamed the science lab. No one paid her any attention. Little did the teacher know she was listening to every word.

She was so clever that she was called the Professor – or 'Prof' for short. At night, when everyone had gone home, she took charge of her own class!

At night, the Prof brought young cats in off the streets and gave them science lessons. It kept them out of trouble. The young cats called themselves the Lab Cats. As each one came in, the Prof marked them off her list.

"Swot, Ginger, Lucky, Basher, Precious…oh dear, Fluff's missing."

8

"Tonight we are going to look at what makes things move. For a start, how can we get this toy train moving?"

"Easy," said Swot. "Give it a push."

The Prof pushed it and, sure enough, it rolled across the table top.

"Good," she said. "Now can you think of another way?"

How does a train engine move its carriages?

"You can pull it," suggested Lucky.

"That's right," said the Prof. "Pushes and pulls — they both make things move. We call them *forces*."

"That's because they *force* things to move, don't they?" added Lucky.

"My turn to play with the train," said Basher, shoving Lucky out of his way. The Prof frowned and grabbed him.

Hey! You pushed me!

Oy! That's my new shirt you're pulling!

She turned to the others. "Basher pushed Lucky. Now I'm pulling Basher. Let's see if you can tell the difference between pushes and pulls."

She showed them some picture cards on a board.

"Have a look at these. Which action is a push, and which a pull?"

Push

Pull

Why not have a try yourself?

Fluff was puzzled. "You said forces make things move. Well, these cats are pulling on the rope, but it isn't moving."

"That's because the cats are pulling in opposite directions," said the Prof, "and the forces are balanced. When one side doesn't pull so hard, the forces won't be balanced. Then the rope will move."

"Now, watch this!" The Prof held up a marble – then let
it fall. "You saw how it speeded up, so where is the force?"

"I can't see any force," Precious pointed out. "No one
pulled or pushed the marble."

"It must be invisible!" declared Lucky, wide-eyed.

"Well done! Any ideas what this invisible force is called?"

"Gravity!" Swot shouted eagerly.

Fluff looked cross. "I was going to say that," he muttered.
"Never mind," whispered Precious. "Swot is showing
off – as usual."
"Yes, the force is called gravity," continued the Prof. "It's
the force that pulls everything down towards the floor –
towards the centre of the Earth."

"The marble has stopped falling," said Basher, looking at the floor. "So has gravity been switched off now?"

"No, no," the Prof said quickly. "Gravity pulls all the time, so it is still pulling the marble down. But now the floor is in the way and stops it falling any further; the floor is pushing the marble up, and so the forces are balanced."

15

"Now let's see what happens when you drop the marble from different heights," said the Prof.

After a few tries, Fluff said, "When you start the marble higher up, it hits the ground faster, doesn't it?"

"It happens too quickly to tell," replied Basher. "Let's slow its fall by making it run down a ramp."

"Good idea," agreed the Prof.

Starting at fifteen centimetres.

They started the marble at different points up the ramp, then measured how far it rolled.

"Look," said Fluff, "when the marble starts higher up, it rolls further. That shows it was going faster at the bottom of the ramp."

"That makes sense," declared Swot. "Gravity has a longer time to pull on it."

"Now see what happens when the blue marble comes down the ramp and hits another marble," said the Prof.

She placed a large red marble at the bottom of the ramp. "I want you to watch how far the blue one makes the red one go."

"Next we shall see what the blue marble will do to this small yellow one," said the Prof. "I shall start the blue one from the same point up the ramp. Why?"

Basher put his paw over Swot's mouth so that Fluff could answer, "Er…so it comes out at the same speed?"

"Well done, Fluff!" said the Prof. "Before you let go, have a guess at what will happen. Will the yellow marble go as far along the table as the bigger red one?"

"It will go further because little things are quicker than big, clumsy things," suggested Fluff.

"No way!" protested Basher. "Big things are stronger than weedy little things."

"Well, let's see," said the Prof. "You can roll the marble down the ramp now, Fluff."

Whoosh! The blue marble hit the small yellow one and knocked it flying.

"So," said Swot, "that means something light is easier to push and moves faster than something heavy."

He made a note of that in his book.

"I've had enough," complained Basher. "I'm hungry. There must be a mouse around here somewhere. I'm off to have a look."

With that, he headed for the door.

"Not so fast!" the Prof called out. "I need you for a little experiment."

"Expurr…iment, did you say?" asked Lucky, sitting comfortably and purring happily.

The Prof grabbed hold of Basher's tail. "If I want something to go faster," she said, "I must push it in the direction it is already moving. If I pull it in the opposite direction — as I am doing to Basher — I will slow it down."

PURRRR

"What else might slow you down?" the Prof asked. "Suppose, for example, you were in a moving car."

"Air!" declared Swot. "A sports car is low and sleek so as to reduce air resistance."

"Quite right!" exclaimed the Prof. "The car has to push its way through the air, and the air pushes back on the car in the opposite direction. We call this slowing-down force *air resistance,* or *drag.* Cyclists crouch low over the handlebars of a bicycle to reduce drag."

Yes, dogs are always getting rides in the back seat.

I know. Why is it always dogs and not cats?

Why do you think planes and rockets are long and thin?

"Air resistance can sometimes be a good thing," the Prof continued. "It's what slows the fall of a parachute."

"Purr…achute, did you say?" asked Lucky, starting to purr once more.

The Prof looked sternly at her.

"Sorry. Can't help myself," murmured Lucky.

The Prof continued. "I want you all to make your own parachutes in different sizes, using these hankies. Tie each corner of the hankie with a piece of thread, then fasten the threads to a coin with sticky tape.

"When you have finished, you can drop your parachutes. Which one do you think will fall fastest?"

"Ginger's small parachute falls faster than my big one!" exclaimed Lucky.

"She's right. Why is that?" asked Ginger.

"Air resistance increases with the size of the parachute," explained the Prof. "The smaller parachute falls faster because it has less surface for the air to resist."

"There's another type of slowing-down force called *friction*," continued the Prof. "It happens when something travels over a surface.

"We let the block fall down the ramp, always from the same point, and let it slide over rough and smooth surfaces – the table top, a tablecloth and sandpaper – then measure how far it slides before it stops."

"The block went furthest when it slid over the table top," reported Ginger. "The next furthest was the tablecloth, and it barely moved at all over the sandpaper."

"So the table top has the least friction," said Swot, "and sandpaper the most."

"Friction stops your shoes skidding," added the Prof. "It also slows down your bike when you put on the brakes."

"Think about this block resting on the table," said the Prof. "What did I say before about forces balancing?"

"Gravity pulling down and the table top pushing up?" suggested Lucky.

"Good. It is the same when I place this block in water. The water pushing it up balances the gravity pulling it down and so the block floats."

She picked up a bunch of keys. "But these keys are heavy," she continued. "The push of the water is not enough to make them float. This time gravity wins: the keys force their way through the water and sink.

"Let's see which of these will float: potato, pencil, stone, eraser, sponge, ice cube, wooden spoon and metal fork."

"Right, Lab Cats, that's all for tonight," said the Prof. "It will soon be morning, and the children will be here."

There were groans of disappointment from all – except Basher, whose eyes lit up at the thought of breakfast.

"See you all next time. Mind how you go," said the Prof, waving them goodbye.

What the words mean

Air resistance: When something, such as a car, moves, it has to push its way through the air. The air pushes back with a slowing-down force called *air resistance* or *drag*.

Floating: Something floats on the surface of water when the upward force of the water balances the downward force of gravity.

Force: A force can make something move or go faster. If the force is in the opposite direction to the thing that is moving, it will make the object slow down.

Friction: Friction is a force that slows things down when they travel over a surface. It sometimes stops things from moving at all.

Gravity: Gravity is the force that pulls things towards the Earth – down towards the floor.

Pull and push: Two kinds of force.

Sinking: Something will sink in water when the upward force of the water is not strong enough to balance the downward force of gravity.

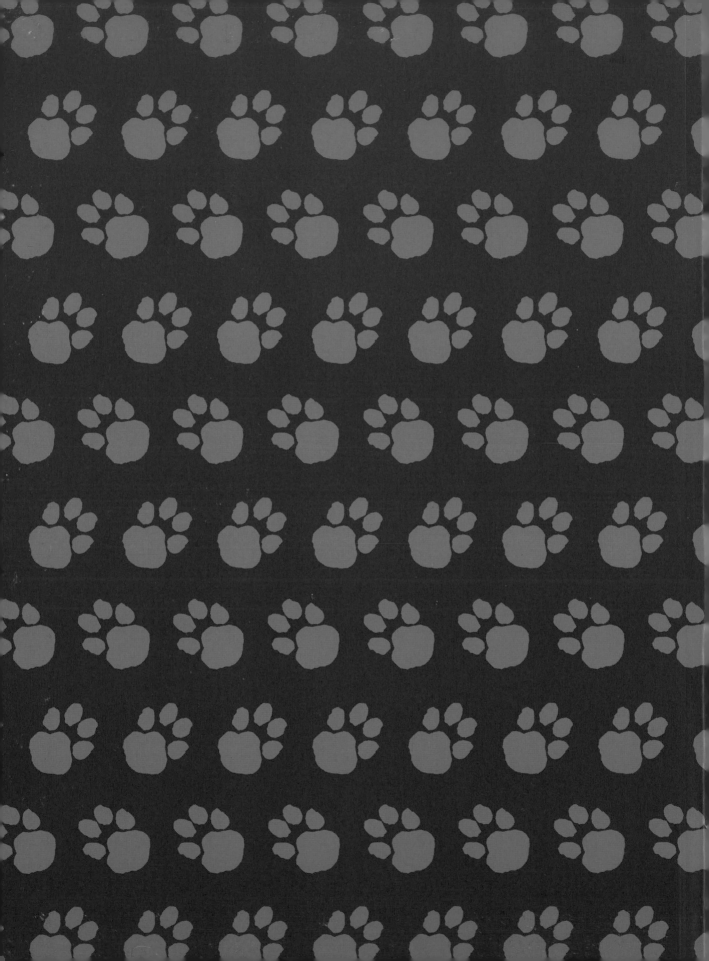